RAINY DAYS
Arts & Crafts

PRINTING
AND
DIECUTTING

VANESSA BAILEY

WATTS BOOKS
London • New York • Sydney

CONTENTS

Design: David West
Children's Book
Design
Designer: Keith Newall
Photography: Roger Vlitos

© Aladdin Books Ltd 1993

Created and produced by
N.W. Books
28 Percy Street
London W1P 9FF

First published in
Great Britain in 1993 by
Watts Books
96 Leonard Street
London EC2A 4RH

ISBN 0 7496 1475 7

A CIP catalogue record for this book
is available from the British Library

Printed in Belgium

Introduction

This book is full of all sorts of printing ideas for you to try out. It introduces you to the various techniques of printing from stamps to screen prints. Find out how to make a letterhead, wrapping paper, designs for T–shirts, wallpaper, your own personalised stamp, and much more.

Some of the projects are quite simple and can be made quickly. Others will take more time and patience. Printing is fun and rewarding, and one of its great advantages is that you don't need a lot of expensive equipment.

When you have tried some of these ideas, why not design your own prints, adding your ideas to what you have learned?

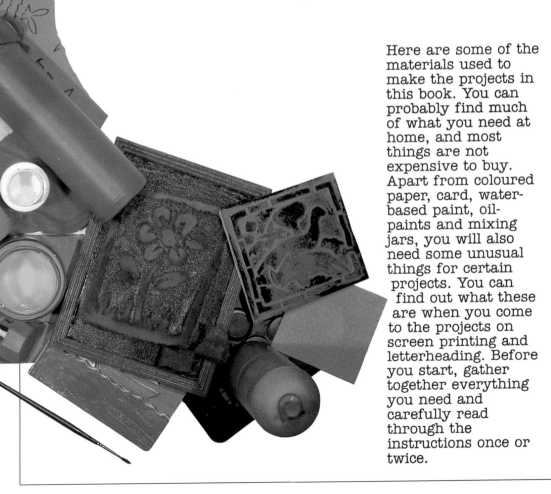

Here are some of the materials used to make the projects in this book. You can probably find much of what you need at home, and most things are not expensive to buy. Apart from coloured paper, card, water-based paint, oil-paints and mixing jars, you will also need some unusual things for certain projects. You can find out what these are when you come to the projects on screen printing and letterheading. Before you start, gather together everything you need and carefully read through the instructions once or twice.

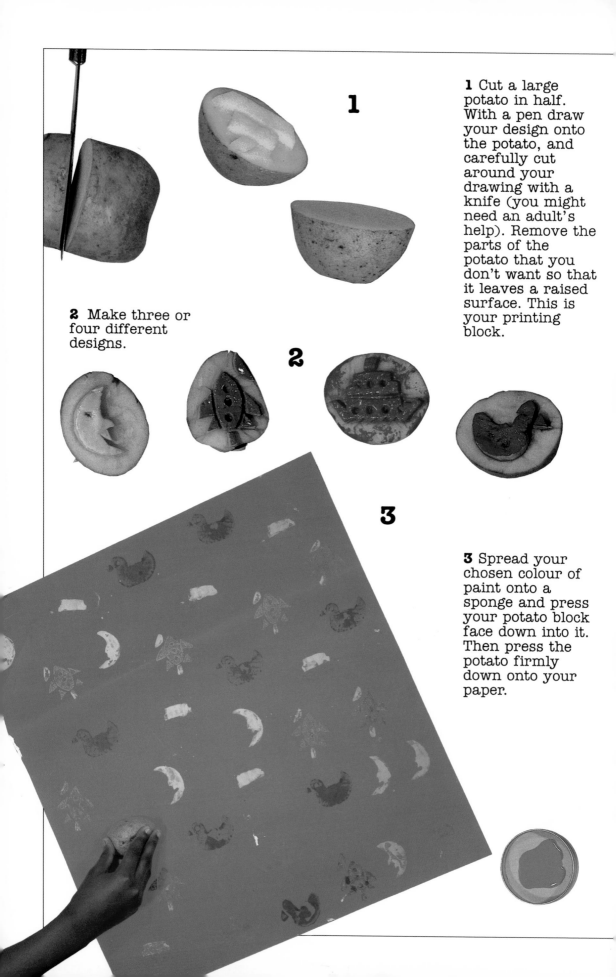

1

1 Cut a large potato in half. With a pen draw your design onto the potato, and carefully cut around your drawing with a knife (you might need an adult's help). Remove the parts of the potato that you don't want so that it leaves a raised surface. This is your printing block.

2 Make three or four different designs.

2

3

3 Spread your chosen colour of paint onto a sponge and press your potato block face down into it. Then press the potato firmly down onto your paper.

4 Repeat the printing so that you gradually build up a colourful pattern. You can experiment with different colours of paint and paper. When you have finished, leave it to dry.

Potato prints

Simple potato prints can be made into very effective wrapping paper. You don't have to be good at drawing as simple shapes can make interesting patterns and are much easier to cut out.

You will need potatoes, a sponge, a pen, coloured paper, poster paints and a knife.

Dino prints

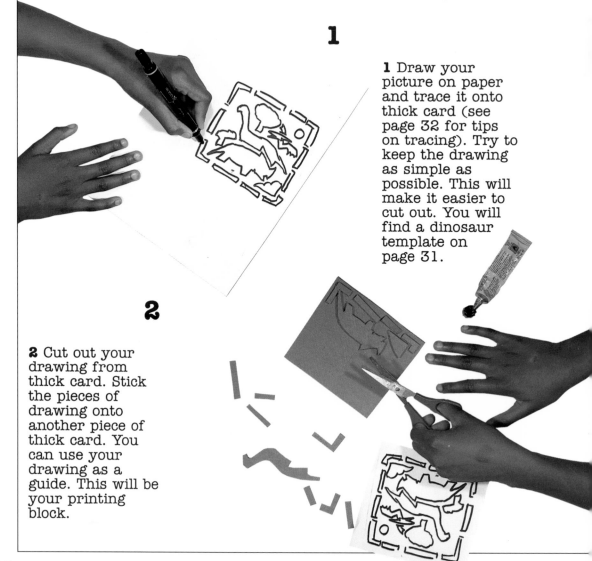

Using thick card is another way of printing from a block. It might take a bit longer than the potato block, but it's just as much fun. Use this method to print greetings cards for your friends and family.

You will need thick card, tracing paper, thin card, poster paints, pencil and scissors. You will also need a roller and tray to transfer the paint evenly onto your printing block.

1

1 Draw your picture on paper and trace it onto thick card (see page 32 for tips on tracing). Try to keep the drawing as simple as possible. This will make it easier to cut out. You will find a dinosaur template on page 31.

2

2 Cut out your drawing from thick card. Stick the pieces of drawing onto another piece of thick card. You can use your drawing as a guide. This will be your printing block.

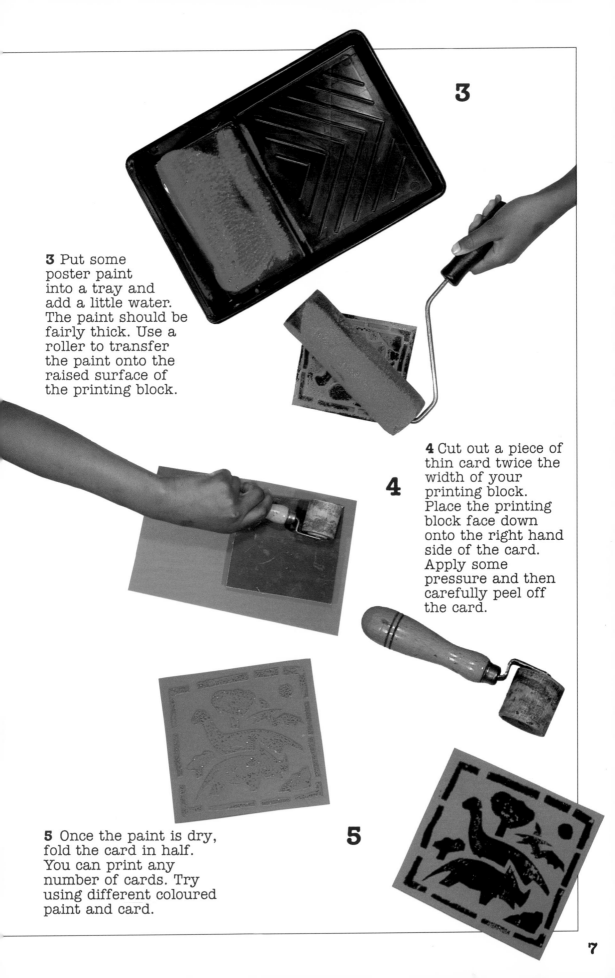

3 Put some poster paint into a tray and add a little water. The paint should be fairly thick. Use a roller to transfer the paint onto the raised surface of the printing block.

3

4 Cut out a piece of thin card twice the width of your printing block. Place the printing block face down onto the right hand side of the card. Apply some pressure and then carefully peel off the card.

4

5 Once the paint is dry, fold the card in half. You can print any number of cards. Try using different coloured paint and card.

5

Junk hanky

Here's a great way to liven up your handkerchiefs (with your parent's permission). The printing technique is the same as in the last two projects, but this time we show how you can use everyday junk to make your printing block. It's fun and cheap to do as well!

You will need handkerchiefs, a roller and waterproof inks or dyes so that the patterns do not wash out in the washing machine. These are easily available at most craft shops. You will also need to collect various bits of packaging, or junk, that have interesting textures or raised surfaces (see below).

1

1 Look around your house for any junk or packaging with an interesting or raised surface for your printing blocks. Shown here is a collection containing cardboard egg-boxes, an old sponge, a baking tin, wool, bottle tops, and lids from plastic containers with raised images on them. Remember you can always make your own printing blocks by cutting out pieces of shaped card, to add to your collection.

2

2 Lay your hanky out flat over a piece of paper or cloth, so that the ink bleeding through will not ruin the work surface. You can either dip your printing block into the ink or use a roller (see page 7). Then press onto the hanky. Repeat this process as many times as you want, using different colours and types of packaging or junk. When your design is finished, leave it to dry.

3

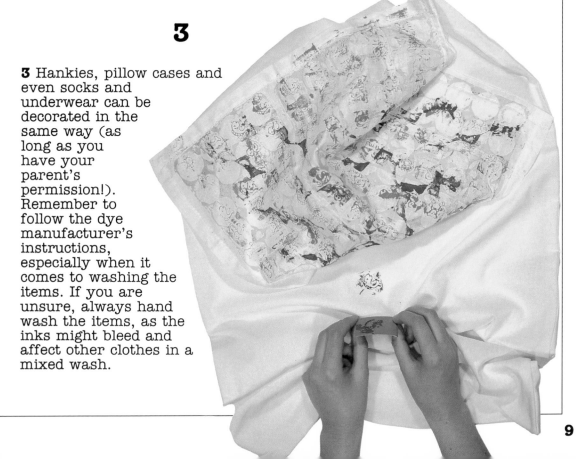

3 Hankies, pillow cases and even socks and underwear can be decorated in the same way (as long as you have your parent's permission!). Remember to follow the dye manufacturer's instructions, especially when it comes to washing the items. If you are unsure, always hand wash the items, as the inks might bleed and affect other clothes in a mixed wash.

Rubber stamp

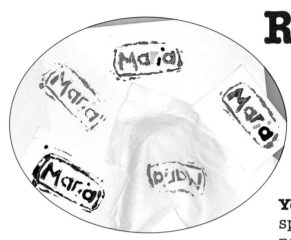

Here's an effective way to make your own personalised stamp. You can stamp stationery or personal items time and again in any colour you want.

You will need some clay, a sponge or paint brush, tracing paper, paint or ink or dye and, most important of all, some rubber latex glue, which goes rubbery when dry.

1

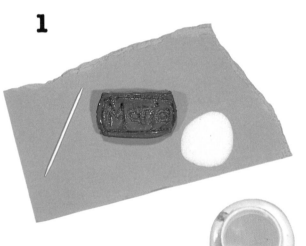

1 Create a mould using clay. Use a toothpick or similar sharp object to indent your name into your clay mould. Make sure the letters are quite thick and not too deep.

2

2 Brush a thin layer of grease into your mould, and fill it in with latex glue. This should be done in several layers, leaving the glue to dry before spreading on a new layer. Keep on applying layers of glue until you have a thickness of about one centimetre.

3 Allow the glue to dry. Carefully peel it off and stick the back of the rubber onto a wooden block. This will make it easier to hold. You will notice that the letters on your mould are in 'mirror' form. When you print, however, the letters will read properly. This is your personalised stamp.

3

4

4 Mix some paint, ink, or dye with a small amount of water in a jar lid. Apply paint to the raised areas of the stamp with a brush or sponge. Press your stamp down firmly onto a piece of paper. Hey presto, your name is in print!

5

5 You can brush on different colours at the same time to give a multicoloured letterhead. Try different coloured paper or small cards that you can give to friends.

Marbled paper

Marbled paper makes an effective and professional surface for covering all sorts of objects. School exercise books and waste paper bins suddenly become interesting objects to look at. And they are very easy to make.

You will need large pieces of thick paper, oil-based paints, a large bowl and turpentine or white spirit.

1 Fill the bowl with water. In several smaller containers, mix some oil-paints with a little turpentine or white spirit. Gently pour the oil-paints onto the surface of the water. The oil-paints will float on the water's surface. Slowly stir until you get a swirly pattern.

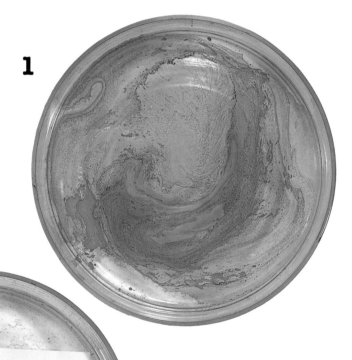

2 Wait for the surface paint to stop swirling. Cut a piece of paper that will fit into the bowl. Carefully place your paper onto the surface of mixed paint and water.

3

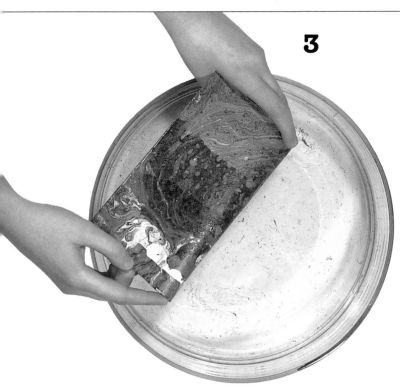

3 Slowly peel the paper off the surface and leave it to dry. The image left on the dried paper should have a marbled effect. If you find the oil-paint is going lumpy or sinking, try using different amounts of paint and white spirit in your mixture. Experiment with different colours and patterns.

4

4 You can use the paper for wrapping presents or for covering your school books or pencil box.

Wax and paint

You have probably found out that trying to draw on waxy or shiny surfaces is extremely difficult, if not impossible. You can use this to your advantage and create some stunning designs to print onto your T–shirts. (Don't forget to get permission!)

You will need a thick black pen, paper, a roller, paint or dye and a candle or wax crayon. You will also need a piece of glass with its edges taped over so as not to cut yourself. Be very careful with it! If you are printing onto material that you have to wash, you must use dyes that will not wash out.

1

1 Think of a pattern you would like to design, and draw it onto paper with a thick black pen.

2

2 Place the glass over your drawing. Using a candle, or crayon, fill in the areas on the glass that are not black. Make sure that you don't go over the black lines. If you do make a mistake, you can easily scrape off the wax with a sharp object.

3

3 Mix your paint or dye to a watery consistency, but make sure the colour is quite strong. Paint across the wax quickly. The paint will run off the wax and settle on the glass where there is no wax.

4

4 While the paint is still wet, place your T-shirt in position over the wax design. Make sure it is quite flat. Press over the T-shirt with a roller, then carefully peel it off. Your print will now be on your T-shirt. Leave it to dry, then you can wear it.

Fishy stencil

Here's an idea to liven up your bedroom with your own personalised wallpaper. Stencils are a great way of repeating an image and are used all over the world, from army vehicle markings to chemistry set symbols used in the classroom.

You will need some thin card, paint, a sponge and a sharp knife or pair of scissors.

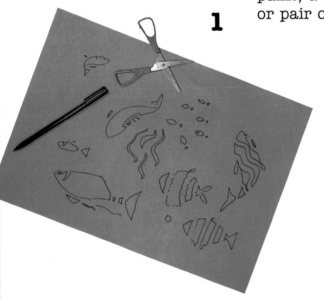

1

1 Draw your design onto a piece of card as shown. You will find some useful templates on pages 30 and 31. When you draw your images, you should bear in mind the parts that are going to be cut out. So keep your images simple. This is why the fish does not have eyes.

2

2 Carefully cut out your design as shown with a sharp knife or pair of scissors. This part is very difficult. **Ask an adult to help you.**

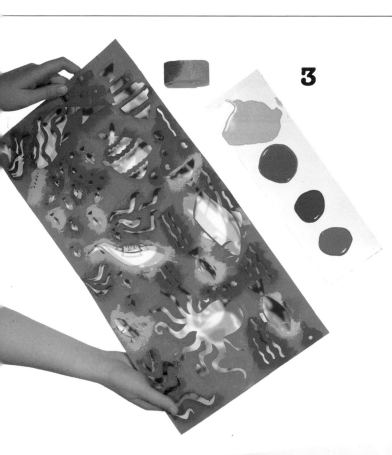

3

3 Next, prepare the sheet of paper you are going to print on. If you are going to cover an area of wall, measure the width of the wall and tape pieces of paper together to the correct length. Cut out a small piece of sponge. Pour small amounts of poster paint onto a saucer.

4

4 Place your stencil over the paper and tape it into position. Now you can apply the paint by dabbing the sponge into the paint, and then onto the paper through the stencil. Complete the whole section before taking the stencil off and placing it over the next section. Let your wallpaper dry before sticking it to the wall. Now your bedroom wall will be bright and cheerful!

Screen printing

Screen printing is often used in the fashion industry to print logos or designs onto material, especially clothes. Here's a great way to liven up old T-shirts with your own creative designs. Make sure you get a parent's permission. If you want the design to stay on the T-shirt, you will have to use waterproof dyes. However, you can use water-based paints which will wash out.

You will need an old picture frame, an old pair of tights and some dyes or paints. You will also need a squeegee (window washer) that is the same width as the frame. A firm piece of card will do if the squeegee is difficult to find.

1

1 Cut out a square from the tights that is slightly larger than the picture frame. Stretch the tights over the frame and secure them using staples. This is your printing screen.

2

2 Draw a picture on paper and place your screen over the drawing (see page 31 for the flower template). Cover the tights with rubber latex glue, leaving spaces where the drawing appears. Leave to dry.

3

3 Place your T-shirt face up and put your screen on top of it. Squirt paint inside the top edge of the screen.

4

4 Place the squeegee at the top where the paint is. Pull it slowly, but firmly, along the length of the screen. The paint will be squeezed through the screen where there is no glue. Lift the screen off gently and see the print on your T-shirt.

1 Draw a picture and trace it onto thick card. A simple image will produce a better print (see page 32 for the template and tips on tracing). Cut out the pieces of card from your picture. Keep the pieces that you want to print.

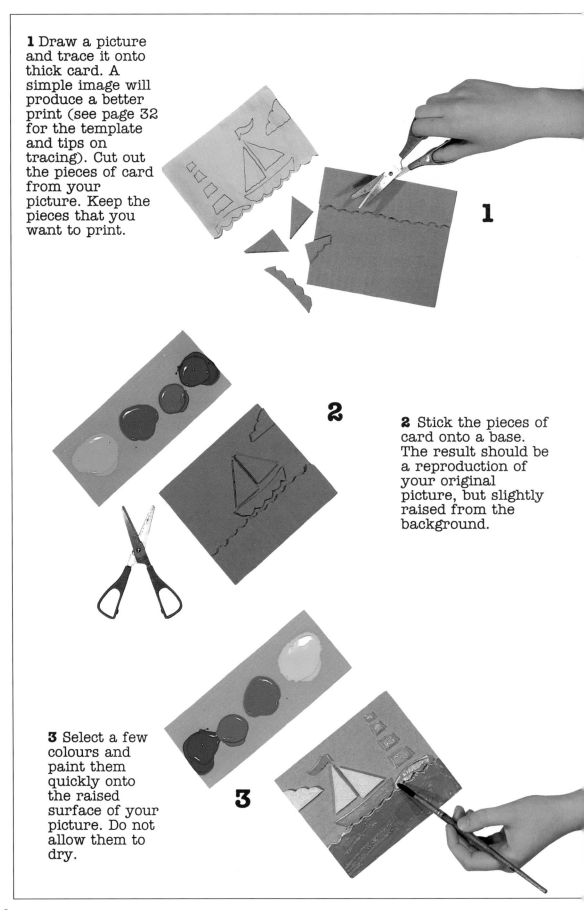

1

2

2 Stick the pieces of card onto a base. The result should be a reproduction of your original picture, but slightly raised from the background.

3 Select a few colours and paint them quickly onto the raised surface of your picture. Do not allow them to dry.

3

4

4 Turn the picture block over and lay it on a piece of paper. Use a roller to press the block firmly onto the paper.

5 Carefully peel the block off the paper. If the print is too faint it means the paint was too dry or there was not enough of it. Experiment with different colours and thickness of paint. You will not get a perfect copy as your picture block does not have a level surface, but some of the results will be very interesting to look at.

5

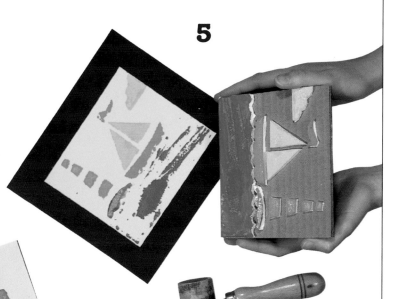

Colour prints

This is an easy method to reproduce several prints using more than one colour. You can have a lot of fun experimenting with different effects and colours. Don't forget to number your finished prints and sign them.

You will need some thick card, a roller, tracing paper, white paper, scissors and paint.

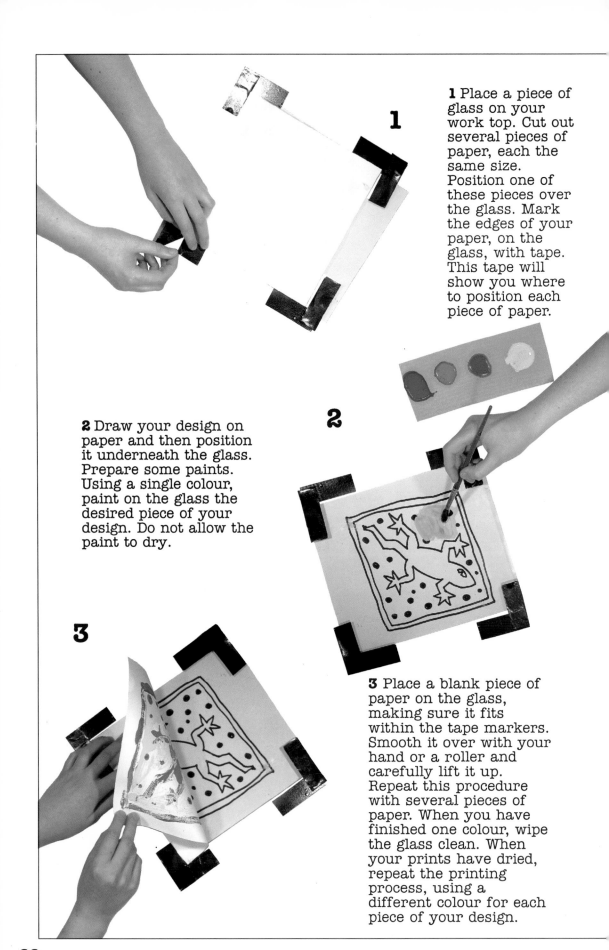

1 Place a piece of glass on your work top. Cut out several pieces of paper, each the same size. Position one of these pieces over the glass. Mark the edges of your paper, on the glass, with tape. This tape will show you where to position each piece of paper.

2 Draw your design on paper and then position it underneath the glass. Prepare some paints. Using a single colour, paint on the glass the desired piece of your design. Do not allow the paint to dry.

3 Place a blank piece of paper on the glass, making sure it fits within the tape markers. Smooth it over with your hand or a roller and carefully lift it up. Repeat this procedure with several pieces of paper. When you have finished one colour, wipe the glass clean. When your prints have dried, repeat the printing process, using a different colour for each piece of your design.

4 You can use this same process on a handkerchief. Mix the paint with some PVA glue to stop it cracking when it dries. This technique is better on cotton and should give you a very good print.

5 The end result will look something like this. You can use as many or as few colours as you want. You will get some new colours when you overlap the colours. For example, the green dots are a result of the blue printing over the yellow.

4

5

Lizard print

Make some limited edition prints on paper or material. With this method of printing, you can build up a full colour picture by printing one colour at time.

You will need tape, colour paints and absorbent paper, or material such as cotton. You will also need a small sheet of glass with the edges taped (see page 14). You will find a lizard template on page 31.

1 Draw your picture on paper, and trace it onto thick card (see page 32 for tips on tracing). You will need to make three printing blocks, one for each colour. Bear in mind how the picture is going to be coloured. For example, if you want a green colour, you need to have that piece on the yellow block and the blue block.

2 To make your printing blocks, label each piece of the drawing with the colours they should be. Cut out the drawing from the card (you may need an adult's help). Stick all the parts that are red onto a base in the correct position, according to your drawing. You can use the trace to check they are correctly positioned. Do the same with the other two blocks.

3 You will now have three printing blocks. Each block will print one colour. When all of the blocks have been printed, they will make up the complete picture. Start with the yellow block. Use a roller to apply the paint to the block. Turn it over and press it down onto a piece of paper.

4

4 Repeat step 3 with the other two blocks, all printing onto the same piece of paper. Finally, your full colour print will emerge. You can make as many prints as you want. Experiment with different colour combinations, and see what colours you can create!

Full colour

When certain colours are mixed together, they make new colours. For example, yellow and blue make green, blue and red make purple, and red and yellow make orange. You can use this to your advantage to make a full colour print with just three colours!

You will need some thick card, a roller, a sharp knife, paper, tracing paper and just three poster colour paints – red, yellow and blue.

Mix and match

Create a limited edition print with some of the printing techniques already used. You can mix and match the various methods as much as you want. What you should end up with is a series of prints that are highly individual.

You will need a sheet of glass, a wax candle, a sponge, thin card, a sharp knife, potatoes, poster paints and paper.

1 Create the background using the glass and wax process used on page 14. Use the wax candle to draw the clouds and sun. Quickly cover the sky area with blue paint and the ground with green. Do not let the paint dry. Place a sheet of paper over the top and press over it firmly with a roller. Peel back the paper and leave it to dry. You can repeat this several times if you are going to make lots of prints.

1

2 Use the stencil process on page 16 to create the details for the picture. Cut out the shapes from thin card for a sun, a house, a hedge and a pond. Dip a sponge into paints and dab it over the cut-outs, onto your background of sky and grass.

2

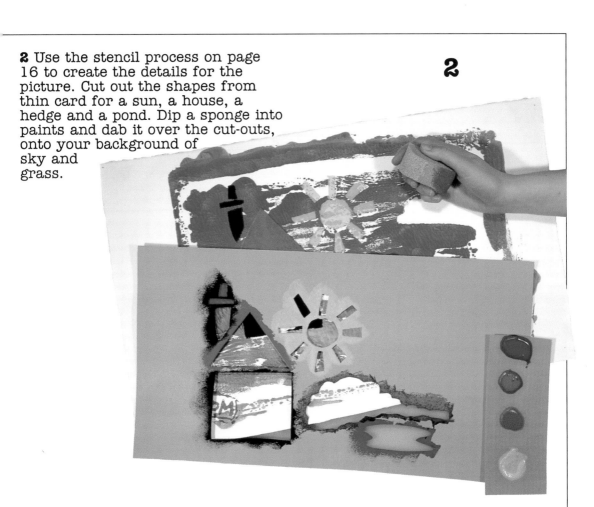

3

3 Use potato blocks to add more detail. See page 4 for potato printing. Cut out simple ducks from the potato, and apply some paint to the surface. Print a couple of ducks. You can use the rubber stamp on page 10 to sign the finished print.

Useful tips

Here are some useful tips when preparing paints. If you find that your print is warping it usually means the paint is too watery. Sometimes it is useful to have watery paints, especially for the glass printing. In these cases it is best to print onto thicker paper or material. Be sure to allow the paint to dry on a print before going on to use the next colour. (However, it is worth experimenting with wet paints for special effects).

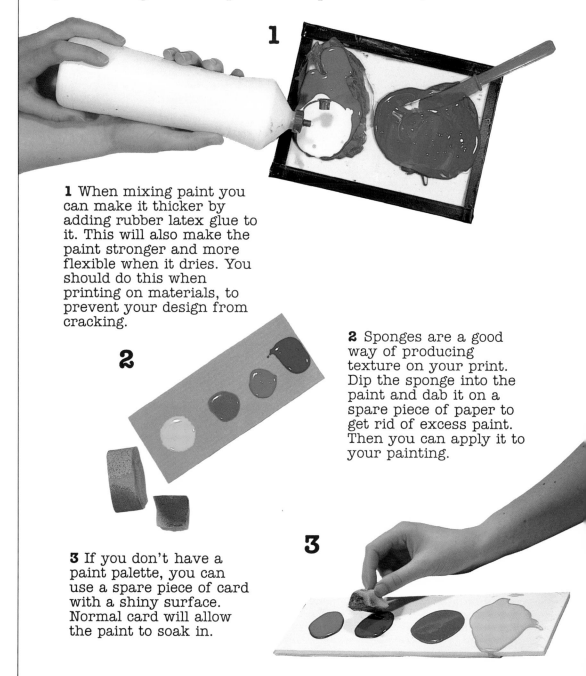

1 When mixing paint you can make it thicker by adding rubber latex glue to it. This will also make the paint stronger and more flexible when it dries. You should do this when printing on materials, to prevent your design from cracking.

2 Sponges are a good way of producing texture on your print. Dip the sponge into the paint and dab it on a spare piece of paper to get rid of excess paint. Then you can apply it to your painting.

3 If you don't have a paint palette, you can use a spare piece of card with a shiny surface. Normal card will allow the paint to soak in.

4 Watery paint is very useful for glass surface printing. Be careful not to make it too watery, or the colour will lose its strength.

5 Some of the projects require the paint to be applied using a paint roller. The paint is first spread into a roller tray, applied onto the roller and then painted onto the design. This technique will produce an even layer of paint and is a lot quicker than using a paint brush.

6 If you don't have any coloured paper you can use the roller to colour white paper. Remember not to water down the paint as it will make the paper warp.

Templates

See page 32 for tracing instructions.

Fish templates P16/17

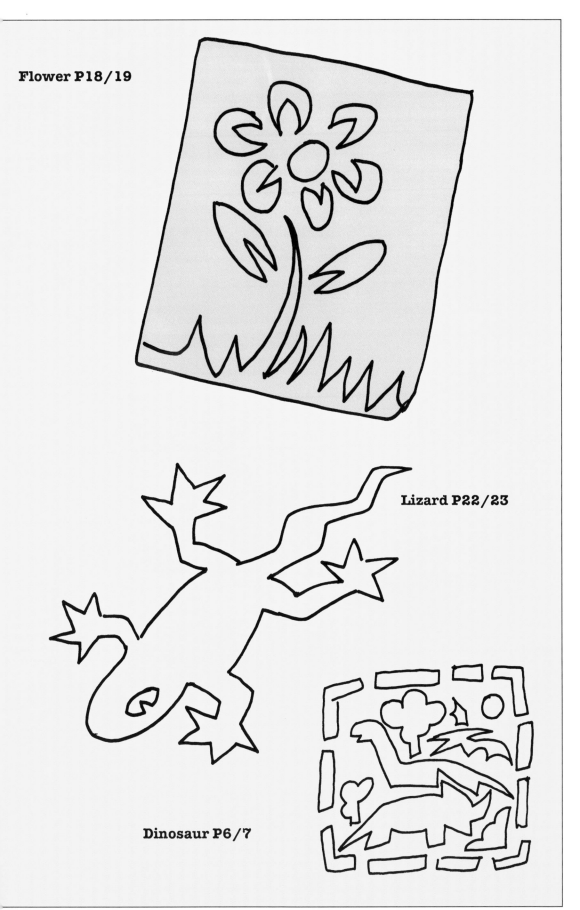

Flower P18/19

Lizard P22/23

Dinosaur P6/7

Templates

You can trace the templates shown here and on the previous pages by following this simple procedure. 1) Lay a piece of tracing paper over the design and hold it in place. 2) Trace the design with a pencil. 3) Take the tracing paper off the book and turn it over. Scribble over the back with a soft pencil. 4) Turn the trace over and position it on a piece of paper. 5) Firmly retrace over the tracing. This should leave a copy of the original on the paper.

Sailing boat P20/21

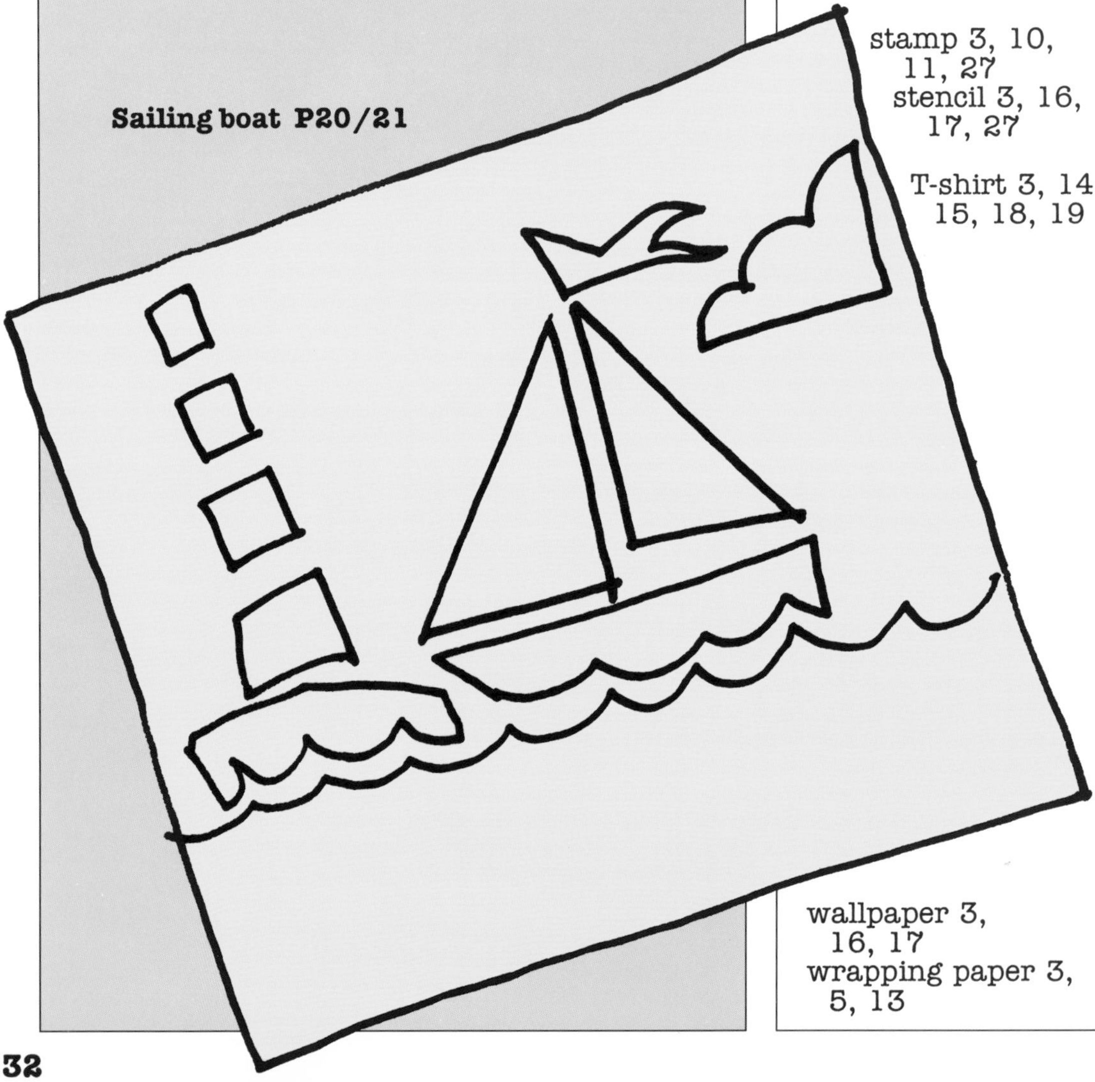

Index